The Insides of Myself - Riley Adora

AF593202

Part One: The Broken

Some days… I'm a little more broken…

The Devil:

The Devil will coat his words in honey and his lips will be sweet and soft
His hands will cradle yours and his eyes will melt you into them
He will show you a world of roses with a river of sweet nectar

And just as you take a step into this world of fantasy
A door slams behind you and there's no escape

He sets it all on fire and you're caught in the middle of it all
Watching as he laughs on his throne of lies and bones
The fire engulfs you as you struggle to breathe
Your skin melting off the bones as you watch him stand up

He walks over to you and touches your face
Silly girl, he says, you never learn
His sickening grin is the last thing you see

Monster:
There are days where I feel okay
Hell, there are days where I feel great

But at night
When the lights are dim and the music of the day slowly fades away
The pain of losing you creeps back in
Like the monster in your closet from when you were seven

Loneliness is a hell of a drug
I can talk and laugh and pretend that everything is okay
But even when I'm with them
Loneliness kicks back in and drags me down

I'm going through withdrawals
This pain is an addiction
I can't let you go

You left me:

You left me
And all I ever wanted was for you to just come back
You left me
And every red rose that grew in my heart had all turned black

And now here you are again
So why am I not happier?
I don't wanna play this game again

If I could let myself slip into the honey you speak
Maybe I would find myself and all that I seek
But the flowers have all died
And my heart is wrapped in thorns
Every night I spent crying and dying
Just waiting for you to come home

You left me
And the house I built for the two of us crumbled to the ground
You left me
All the windows are now cracked and you couldn't hear a sound
You left me
I wish that I could hear the voice of reason
But with every passing season
I can feel you slipping through my fingertips

Sleepless:

12 AM

I am awake in my bed

I should be sleeping, resting for the day to come

But I can't

I can't stop thinking about every mistake I have ever made

The rain is starting to drizzle

1 AM

I should be sleeping

Instead, I think about him and how I wish he was here

I think about whether or not its worth it to be so many miles away

I think about if he would love me the same way in person

The rain is really starting to come down now

2 AM

I shouldn't be awake right now

I keep thinking of how I let my parents down

Of every dream they had for me and how I crushed it with a few simple words

I think about how my dad looks at me with disappointed eyes and a tired heart

It's pouring now

3 AM

I have to go to sleep now

I can't keep staying awake like this

The shadows in the darkness are becoming more real

The crawling is sinking deeper into my skin

The dark thoughts are becoming louder and stronger

It sounds like there's a hurricane outside now

4 AM

...

Taken:

You might have taken my innocence,
but you will never take my smile
- Burn in hell, you monster

When I lost you:

It felt like thousands of stars were falling from the sky and this time there was no time for wishes
Like the oceans were rising and there was no stopping them until they drowned everything in their way
It was as if the moon herself hid and never came back out for fear of what might happen
That's what it felt like when I lost you

Bad Habit:
Like a cigarette pressed against my lips
You were just another bad habit I couldn't quit

Lost:
Did you mean it when you said you loved me?
Did you mean it when you said you didn't anymore?
- I guess I'll just stay lost in your words

You:

You'll always be in everything I do
You'll be the wind in my hair on a stormy spring day
The shivers that crawl up my spine when the air is cold and crisp
The silent, small ache in my heart on Valentine's day
It'll always be you

I thought about you:

I thought about you

I was consoling a friend the other day
I told her that you never really stop loving someone
And I thought of you

I thought of how easy it was to be your friend
It was effortless, like walking or breathing
I thought about how we got closer and how you told me you loved me
How everything fell apart one last time and we didn't put it together again

I thought about every boy I've ever loved and how none of them ever quite fit the same mold that you did
I thought about how I made you think that there was a chance we could be together, even though I always knew that he was a whole new mold that I preferred much more
I thought about how you called me screaming and crying because "How could you just up and disappear from me like that?"
I thought about how you had every chance in the world and you took none of them
I thought about how he took the first chance he had because he knew that we would be amazing together
I thought about how you and I had only ever been best friends
I thought about how I never really thought we could ever be more than that

I thought about how I loved you, but maybe not in the way that I think I did at first
I thought about how a part of me still loves you and always will
I thought about how I love him more than I have ever loved anyone else in my life
I thought about how he knows me better than you ever did because he was willing to break down walls to find out who I really am

I thought about how much better off we both are staying away from each other
I thought about how much pain it would cause everyone involved, how much pain pain it did cause
But most importantly,

I thought about you

Lunch Table:

Sometimes I'm still that scared little girl in the guidance counselor's office
Feeling so alone and like everyone I thought I meant something to
Just up and left me behind
Called me annoying, a mistake, told me I wasn't good enough

No amount of friends at 26 can ever fill the empty lunch table that little girl sat at
She's still there, tears running down her face, sitting in the bathroom stall
Trying to catch her breath, as she can hear the girls laughing outside

Today that little girl has grown up, she no longer sits at the lunch table alone
But some days, the little girl seeps through the cracks as she quietly cries herself to sleep
Feeling nothing but alone, a stranger in the world, a lost cause
Feeling like I'm still that sad little girl sitting alone at the lunch table

Coffee Cups and Cigarettes:

The day drags on and on
Every second takes a little longer to pass by
I can feel the weight of the world on my shoulders
And my chest begins to tighten

I look around my room and all I see are
Coffee cups and cigarette butts
Lost hopes and dreams
Wasting away on shelf in the back of my mind

The wave of anxiety washes over me
And all I can think of is the what ifs

The burn of the bottle in the back of my throat
The room begins to spin and the colors seem to fade
The tears start rolling down my cheeks
And I can feel the elephant in the room

The crushing feeling in my heart
The looks of all the ghosts of my past
Haunt me like grinning monstrosities
Chasing me down the corridors of my mind

Every turn leads me to another wave
Every step feels like I'm sinking
I'm trying to outrun these thoughts
But they're too fast to keep away from

I try to stop it
I try to breathe and fight them back
They're too strong and I fall to the ground
Every single breath is a gasp for air

It feels like I'm choking on my own blood
I can't breathe
I want these feelings to go away
I want to be free from these beings in my head

The room stops spinning
The colors return
The fight is over for now
And I can finally continue my collection

Of coffee cups and cigarettes

The Man in Black:

She sat curled in her bed, tears streaming down her face

Her heart ached and her head hurt

No one cared about her, she said

Her parents never took her cries for help seriously

Her friends forgot about her just as easily

So she laid in her bed clutching her chest

She couldn't breathe

She couldn't see

She was so tired

She just wanted relief

That's when the man in black came

He crawled across the bed slowly to her

He lifted her head and laid it softly in his lap

He stroked her hair and whispered

"Come with me and I promise, you will be free

You will be happy"

He picked her up into his arms and graced her cheek with his hand

"All it takes is a kiss"

His words were dipped in honey

His voice soft and gentle

He was a beautiful man with a warm smile

She wanted to be free

She wanted to be happy

She slowly kissed the man in black

And he turned from the beautiful man to a hideous monster

With jagged teeth and sunken eyes

He grabbed her by the neck

He ripped out her soul

He left nothing but a husk on the floor

Part Two: Heartbreak

You were honeysuckle and sunshine
But she was my whiskey and cigarettes
~~~I'm sorry I couldn't let her go

The Way:

The way her hair fell around her shoulders, like a peaceful waterfall
The way her eyes glimmered in the moonlight as our faces grew closer and closer
The way her lips felt like velvet and tasted like candy
The way the knot in my stomach grew after she told me she loved me
The way my heart stopped beating for a moment, only to restart faster
The way I longed to be her everything
The way I woke up from this beautiful dream
The way I looked at my empty bed, with my eyes full of tears
The way I remember hearing my father say "That's unnatural!" when he saw two females kissing on TV
The way I felt the knot in my stomach sink and make me feel sick
The way the guilt took over my mind
The way she smiled at me in the coffee shop today
The way her lips curved as she asked if she could sit with me
The way she sat, so interested in what I was reading
The way she spoke softly and quickly
The way I wanted to hold onto her, because this was not a dream and I couldn't bear to lose her again
The way she caressed my face on our three month anniversary
The way she told me I was her everything
The way she made me feel whole
The way she didn't make me feel guilty about who I was
The way she loved me

Sunshine:

They're like sunshine on a cold cloudy day
I just wanna stand under them and feel their warmth
And when it starts to rain and they disappear again
I just wait for the day that they come back and I can stand in their embrace again

Stairs:

Why did you wake me up so goddamn early?
Just to fix the stairs of your broken heart
Like I was some kind of contractor ready with all my tools
To fix what's broken inside of you

And I tried, oh boy did I try
But the fact of the matter is no matter how hard I tried
How much I hammered and sawed and drilled away
There were just too many broken pieces for me to put back together

Like a puzzle that just kept falling apart no matter how much glue I used
It felt like your heart was just something that was meant to be broken
The only person that could fix these broken pieces

The only person with the right tools to fix all that's broken
Is you

I can try and try and try over and over again
But nothing I do will fix the you that's broken

And I know that maybe you think someone out there will have the right tools
But they'll just be stuck in the same position as I am
Hammering and sawing and drilling away
Looking for some kind of resemblance to heart that's whole

So I ask you
Please get up and try to fix these broken stairs
I'll be by your side as you do, but only you can fix the broken that's inside of you

Addiction:

The clock goes tick tock, tick tock
Every second passes like an eternity
We pull out our phones and scroll through endless feeds

Of people we wish we looked like
Of places we wish we could go
Of scenarios we wish would happen to us

Addiction is a powerful thing
Even when you're staring it in the face
You don't realize the power it holds over you
You don't realize how it's affecting you

A few minutes pass and you pick it up again
Next thing you know it's been an hour
and you don't remember a thing that has happened
The claws are so deep in you that you struggle to breathe
It feels like something is missing from your life

We become so focused on likes and comments and retweets
From people we don't even know
Their acceptance of us, their approval
We seek it daily and it consumes us

We stare at a screen for so much of ours lives
That we forget to actually live
We forget the people that love and care about us
We lose focus on the things that really matter
So, put down the phone

Live in the moment
And just breathe

Venom:
Sometimes it's a vicious cycle that you've got to break
All that's ever done is just take and take
Giving isn't a word that we know how to do
Instead, we just start spitting venom down each other's throats

Are we addicted to the pain? The poison?
Just keep running in circles
Looking for somewhere to hide
Till the storm subsides and the clouds part

Its like fire in my veins
Like I'm drowning under the weight of the pressure of this love
Its like we just stopped caring

5 years gone like that
And then like a rubber band
We snap back together
And the cycle beings anew

Running around this cycle until one of us falls to the ground
The winner stands above victorious
The loser groveling at their feet
Like every once of love that was once there disappeared

And so it goes over and over again

Bittersweet Memory:

There was a day that I would have put you above anything
A day where you would message me and everything else came to a screeching halt
I would keep my phone with me at all times just waiting for the familiar ding of our friendship
Your name was scratched into my heart like two high school sweethearts' initials on a park bench
Every day I watched and I waited for the moment when I might be put into a place of a certain familiarity with you
But, deep down I knew that he already held that spot and even with all the wishing stars and candles lit, I would never be
Yet, the flame never died out
It kept flickering in the empty cavern of my heart
Your name, still lit, on the rock walls I've built, by the wavering light of my passion
Then there came a day when a harsh reality sunk in
You didn't need me anymore
I was just a sweet memory from long ago and no matter how hard I tried
You would never need me again
I don't blame you
I don't blame him
I don't blame them
It was just harsh reality where you and I were no longer you and I
And instead, we became a bittersweet memory, in the lockbox with your name on it, in the back of my mind

Medicine:

I need my medicine
Not the pill kind you take with a glass of water to help you get better
I need the kind that burns as it runs down your throat and warms you from the inside out
I need the kind that makes you feel fuzzy and numbs any feelings inside
The kind that makes you throw every care to the wind
Making you dance like no one is watching, because well no one is
It's 7 pm and you're in your apartment all alone
The kind that makes you stumble across the living room floor as you try not to vomit on your freshly cleaned carpet
The kind that causes you to break down in the shower
Tears streaming down your face as your chest squeezes your lungs so tightly you feel like you're having a heart attack
You somehow make it to the couch in the living room, because the bed is just too far away and you're in too much pain
You can't see straight and the room starts spinning again
The tears come back and you're in this downward spiral of over-thinking
You try to text her but nothing sounds right
And the next thing you know,
It's the morning
Your head is killing you and you don't remember the night before
You don't remember all the pain you felt or the fact that every time you thought about her your chest got tighter
So, yeah. I need my medicine.
Not the pill kind that helps you get better.
I need the kind that makes me forget about you.

Broken Bones:
You know, part of me always knew I had no chance
I knew that no matter what I did
you loved him and I was no match for that
It just sucks because even after everything
I came back
I knew better, but I came back anyway
You moved on
You don't need me anymore
You don't even talk to me anymore
It's my fault for being so ignorant
For loving you when I knew the feeling would never return to me
I chose to fall for you anyway
And when I finally hit the ground
It felt like every bone in my body broke all at once
And yet, there's a small thought in the back of my mind that refuses to let you go
It says "no. just give it time. she will return to me. she has to."
But I know that's not true
And yet, here I am hoping anyway
And because of that
All these broken bones will never heal

The Way She Liked It:

She always falls asleep with one leg curled up into her stomach and one outstretched

She looks like Spiderman climbing a building, but she's just climbing her way into a dream

I tried sleeping like that once, it wasn't very comfortable and I couldn't pop understand why, but that's just how she likes it

In the morning as we sit, sipping our morning tea, she puts in a teaspoon of cinnamon

Says it makes her think of fall with her family when she was young

I tried drinking my tea like that one day, it didn't really taste very good, but that's just the way she likes it

She sleeps with the window exactly 2/3 of the way open

She says all the way open makes it too cold, but only 1/3 doesn't let enough of the breeze in

She says that the nighttime breeze carried away the bad dreams and carried in the good ones

I tried opening and closing the window and I couldn't notice a difference, but that's just how she liked it

Our divorce was finalized, yesterday

Now, I sleep like Spiderman, drink cinnamon in my tea, and sleep with the window exactly 2/3 of the way open

Why?

Because that's just the way she liked it

Part Three: Hell Of A Drug
Sadness is a hell of a drug
You never really know who you are without it
And the moment it goes away
You crave it again

Anixety:
I can't think straight
The room is spinning and I can't see straight enough to type this
It feels like I'm losing my mind
My head is spinning and my heart is racing

I'm trying to see and straighten my eyes
I can feel the fogginess overcoming my brain and taking up every crevice
I can barely hold my eyes open anymore
The weight of my anxiety and fear are overcoming my sense and I lose control of myself

Rain:
I remember growing up
I'd run outside at the first sight of a storm
I'd dance and spin around as the rain pelted my face
My clothes drenched in the spirit of my childhood

Now, I'm 25 and my clothes still get drenched
But rather than it being from the beautiful rain
It's from the sadness that overflows from my eyes
And stains my shirt with drops of crystals

Just like Alice drowning in the ocean of her own making
I swam around to find some hint of land
To rescue me from drowning in my own tears

Tsunami:
Do you know what it's like to have the whole world falling apart in an instant?
To feel like everything is crashing down around you?

Do you know what it's like to suddenly feel like you don't want to live anymore?
To feel like you will never be good enough and that you'd rather just die?
That everyone would be better off without you?
Someone looks at you funny or changes their tone and you lose your sanity
"They hate me." "I'm not good enough." 'Why are they even friends with me? I'm worthless."

The sadness feels like grief
The anger feels like blinding rage
The happiness is like winning the lottery
And all of that can change in an instant.

I can be happy and full of life
But the moment one small thing goes wrong
The world burns
The universe collapses

And in that moment, you know it's wrong
You know you're overreacting
But you can't stop a tsunami

You hide away and wait for the wave to finish crashing down on everything you know and love
And then you clean up the aftermath

Sanity:
I can feel it
Slipping slowly through my hands like sand
Do you know what it feels like?
To question your own sanity?
It started small
Hearing things that no one else heard
Constantly looking over my shoulder
Now I can't tell if things really did happen or if I dreamed them
My brain feels like its walking through a constant maze
Trying to navigate through fact or fiction
Trying to scream out for help but no one is there to listen
My sanity is slipping...

Do you?
How do you explain the immense pain of your own mind to someone who's never experienced it before?
Do you explain the feeling of someone crushing your heart while it's inside your chest?
Or the jackhammer that gets taken to your head?
How about the floods coming from your eyes that no matter how many breathing exercises you do?
Do you explain how the only thing you can think of is that you'd be better off dead?
Or about how you constantly tell yourself how sad people would be if you were gone but the empathy you once felt is gone?
Do you explain that every day is a constant battle inside your own head and every single thing that goes wrong feels like a shaken-up soda bottle being opened with no way to stop it?
Do you explain that you know the way you're acting is unreasonable, but there's no way to stop it?
Do you explain that every day is exhausting and every breath you take is pain?

Part Four: The Healing
I sit out and look at the sunset
And for a moment, there is a calm...

Sword:

And one day
She realized she didn't need a prince to save her
Through heartbreak and pain
She forged the sword she needed to cut through the chains that kept her held captive

Mask:

She was the type of girl to hide behind a smile
Every day she put on the mask and walked around like everything was fine
She would laugh and joke
But no one knew what she hid underneath

One day though the mask started to crack
Under the weight of the world
She tried to stop the mask from breaking
Afraid of what the world would think

Little by little the crack grew bigger
Until finally it broke in half
Unable to mask her feelings
She broke down

Sobbing, she begged the world to bring back her mask
The world whispered to her
You are stronger than the mask
Once she realized her power
She was unstoppable
Like a phoenix rises from the ashes
She became something stronger

Power:

You could stop a hurricane in its tracks
The power you have inside is stronger than any force on this earth
Take the reigns and harness it for the better
Remember you are made of stardust and magic

Love, Kindness, and Patience:

I'm sorry for all the negative energy I brought to you
I'm sorry for always telling you that you weren't good enough
I'm sorry for always putting other people before you
I'm sorry for making you feel like you could never be enough
I watched all these beautiful women and wished you would look like them
I looked in the mirror and thought you were too big, had too many stretch marks
When the lights were out and his hands were wandering
Every time he touched you, my heart stopped
I was so worried about what others thought about you
I was so worried that others would look at you with disgust
But, I'm sorry...
You deserved love, kindness, and patience
You have been going through so many changes
And I never stopped to think about how my thinking was affecting you
I never thought that after everything we've been through that you would need more from me
But, I promise from here on out
That I will choose to love you for everything you are
and aren't
I will only speak to you with love
I will not let others tell me how you should look
Or how you should act
I will no longer be embarrassed by who you are
I will only treat you how you should be treated
And should have been treated this whole time
With love, kindness, and patience...

I’m not broken:

Just because I'm different
Doesn't mean I'm not worthy
Worthy of love
Worthy of happiness

Don't push your books on me
I don't need your holy water
I won't change
I'm all I need to be

You act like I just woke up one day
And decided to be this way
You say we're made in his image
Then why did you turn away from me

If God is so perfect and loving
Why would he let me be in such misery
For just being me
And loving who I love

I remember crying for years
All because you pushed me away
But now I'm stronger and now I know
I don't need your sympathy

I'm not broken
I'm not lost
I am just who I need to be
And that has always just been me

Part 5: The Love
I never thought I'd find you…

You Chose Me:

I've never been very good with words
But I'm hoping my point comes across

When you look at me its like the whole world stops
And the stars start shining like spotlights in your eyes
Its like the moon and the sun dance in circles above us

When you kiss me, it feels like warmth and comfort
It feels like safety and love

When you hold my hand it feels like I found my missing puzzle piece
Like every wrong turn and bad decision suddenly became irrelevant because I have you
It was as though every step I took, every decision I made, every mistake
Became whispers of the past that all led me here to you

All of the heartache and pain
And the worst and best parts of me all came together to say "Here you go"
And they put you into my life

Every day I thank the universe for giving me you
Every day I thank you for choosing me
You could have had anyone you wanted and yet
You chose me

My annoying, ridiculous, overly emotional dumbass
And you keep choosing me every day
Through good and bad and thick and thin
For every sick day, every disagreement
Every mistake and every win
You keep choosing me
And for that, I will forever be grateful

The Quiet:

We live in a quiet house
In a quiet neighborhood
I used to hate the quiet

But ever since I met you
The quiet doesn't seem so lonely

The quiet used to bring back old memories
And old heartbreaks

But ever since I met you
The quiet doesn't seem so sad

The quiet let the darkness creep in
And let the monsters take over

But ever since I met you
The quiet doesn't seem so scary

Maybe:

Maybe it was the way you made me laugh and the rest of the world just melted away

Like an ice cream cone on a hot summer day, with the sand between your toes and the stickiness between your fingers
Maybe it was the way you could look at me and know exactly what I was thinking before I even said it
Maybe it was the way your eyes lit up whenever you talked about something you were passionate about
Like stars twinkling in the night sky when the moon is dark and the stars are all you see

And they're beautiful, like hundreds of images of your eyes against the dark sky
Maybe it was your laugh
The sound of happiness and joy that filled my ears and opened up my heart to love
The way a little kid sounds when they're playing with their favorite toy or the way that an old man reacts to seeing his grandchild for the first time

Maybe it was the way you held me in your arms, safe and sound like the way a child feels in a parent's embrace
Like nothing could hurt me and the world didn't seem so bad afterall
Maybe it was all of these things that made me fall in love with you
It started slowly, then all at once

And to be honest, I'm not sure that I ever stopped falling
Like Alice down the rabbit hole, it feels like it could go one forever
And I'm okay with that
Because maybe, just maybe, it was always meant to be you

Christmas Wish:

Such a simple question
And maybe when I was younger I would have had an immediate answer
Some kind of toy or new gaming console
Something that I would use for a few days and then forget about it

Now that I'm older there are lots of things that I want
There are lots of things that I need
But none of it seems worthy of being the answer to such a question
Because the truth is, what do I want? What do I really want?

Is to hug you for the last time
To hear your laugh and watch your smile light up the room
Its to sit next to you once more
Watching some soap opera that I don't understand

What do I want?
To be able to say goodbye
To be able to be in your arms as you stroke my hair and tell me it's okay
I want to say I love you one more time and hear it back instead of the echos of silence I'm used to

Happiness:

You remind me of honeysuckle on a warm summer afternoon
Or marshmallows over an open fire on a cool fall night

You are like cotton candy and ferris wheels
Candy canes and Christmas trees

You're like the feeling of sand between my toes on a sunny seaside
Or the comfort of my favorite blanket fresh out of the dryer

Like the moon shining bright surrounded by stars in the dark night sky
The way the sun feels when its shining on your face

You feel like watching the first leaves of autumn falling gracefully on the sidewalk
Or the snow gently covering the horizon on the first day of winter

The first flower pushing through the snow to bloom in Spring
The way a little kid laughs as they fly their first kite on a windy summer day

You remind me of happiness

A Sneak Peek at my next book:

Happy Memories:

I was talking to my mom today
And I remembered that although
Things were not always the best
There were happy memories too

My earliest memory
Was when I was small
It wasn't a birthday party, no
But it was something

I remember the cake
I remember them singing to me
The Barney song
I love you, you love me

I remember when I was a little older
There had been a hurricane
And the little dirt road we lived on
Was covered in mud

My dad and I jumped into our buggy
And rode around at top speeds
Waves of mud flying over us
My mom refusing to let us back in the house

I remember my sister's wedding
There was fun and dancing
I remember my light blue dress
And my hair wrapped in tight little curls

I remember meeting my first crush there
He was just some boy
But I thought about him for years after
Even though he made fun of my teeth

I remember going to my oldest sister's house
Their pantry always stocked to the brim with the best snacks
She had made my favorite dinner

And I threw up all over my favorite pjs when I ate too much

Sure,
Times weren't always the best
But that doesn't mean
There weren't happy memories, too

First Loves:

I think about all the ways you made me laugh
But then I think about all the ways you made me cry

They say first loves never fade away
But, I disagree

Because when I look at him,
I think of all the ways he makes me laugh
Not of all the ways you made me cry

Proud:

*I used to let what others thought of me
Tear me down and bring me to tears*

*I used to think I could never be good enough
That none of what I had done
Would ever make you proud of me*

*This year I have accomplished so much
I have gone above and beyond my wildest dreams
And I know it will only go up from here*

*I don't need you to be proud of me
Because I am proud of myself
I don't need your opinions of who I am
Because my opinion of myself is the only thing that matters*

*At the end of the day
It does not matter what or how you think of me
Because at the end of the day
I am proud of me*

Forever:

*When someone looks at you and says "I love you"
It does not always mean forever*

*You looked at me with stars in your eyes
And hope in your heart*

*You looked at me like everyone else faded away
And it was only you and I left standing
On this little rock we call earth*

*Then one day
The stars faded from your eyes
There was only desolation in your heart
A once empty place, became a crowded room*

When someone looks at you and says "I love you"
It does not always mean forever

Don't Leave:

I sit here in this small empty room
And I think of all the ways you could leave me
But only one could break my heart

We could fight
You could pack your things and leave
You could finally be fed up with my attitude
And decide it was too much for you

You could finally see me for what I am
And decide that I am too much
Too much for you to handle

But there is one way
You could leave
That would break my heart forever
And I would never recover from

You could suddenly disappear from me
I could never get to say goodbye
I might never get to kiss you again or say I love you
All because in an instant you were gone

Please if you ever have the choice
To leave me by packing your things and going
Or to leave me by not saying goodbye
Please choose to the first option

Because
As I sit here in this small room
I think about all the ways you could leave me
And only one would break my heart

Hana:

The moment you walked into my life
Is a moment I will never forget
You have saved me from myself
And I know you will never leave me

You have always had a feisty side
But you have always been by mine

I know there will come a day
When you are no longer here
On that day there will be a hole in my heart
Too big for anything to fill

Because the moment you walked into my life
Is a moment I will never forget

A poem of self love:

She likes her coffee with lots of cream and sugar
She has to sleep by 9:30 or she'll be too tired the next day
She loves cats, but raccoons are her favorite animal
She always locks her car 3 times just to be sure

She's got little freckles across her nose
And on her shoulders
Scattered like stars in the sky

She's got gorgeous green eyes with starbursts of brown
They look like galaxies captured inside her soul
And her tummy is squishy and warm
Her heart is as big as it gets
She will sacrifice everything
If it means making someone else happy

She is learning to love herself
All her good parts
All her flaws
And the in betweens

Forgotten Memory:

I'm not ready
To become a distant thought
A forgotten memory

I see how you look at her
You used to look at me like that, too
I see how you smile when you talk to her
You used to smile at me too

I know I said I moved on
But everywhere I turn I see your face
In windows of the shops on the street
In the shadows of my now empty apartment

I try so hard to move on
I say I'm fine
But I can't let you go
I can't become

A distant thought
Or
A forgotten memory

Let me down slowly:

I see the way your eyes light up when you talk to her
I see the small smile on your face
The way you turn and look at me
With guilt written all over your blank expression

You looked at me with a truth to tell
I know its coming
I try to ignore the pain growing in my chest
Just please, let me down slowly

Lies:

Maybe you could just lie to me
Hold me in your arms
And tell me you love me just one last time

It's killing me to watch you go
If you could live in my heart for just one minute
Maybe then you'd feel the pain I'm going through
The pain of losing you

Was it?:

Was it something I did?
Could I have stopped this?
Why was I not enough for you?

I tried so hard to be everything you wanted
I changed so much about myself
Just to trying to keep you around
Trying so hard to be enough for you

Maybe I'm just not good enough
Maybe the other girls were prettier
Smarter
More interesting

You have no idea what you've done
Sitting on the bathroom floor
My mom in the other room
Debating on ending my life

All I ever wanted was to be enough for you
Guess I'll never be enough for you

Initials:

Your initial hanging around my neck
The same way it's wrapped around my heart
It's how I know I belong to you

My name wrapped around your finger
The same way I'm wrapped around your heart
It's how I know you belong to me

Intertwined like snakes
Two hearts beating as one
Hands touching hands
Body against body

I fell for you like raindrops
Slowly sprinkling the ground
And then
Flooding the streets

Keep:

I kept you like an addiction I couldn't quit
But you didn't keep me at all…

Friends:

I think I'm falling in love with you
The way you smile
The way you laugh

I don't wanna ruin what we have
I know how complicated it gets
When you become more than friends

Are we really just friends though?
Friends don't look at each other
Like we do

Friends don't talk to each other
Like we do

We say its just being friendly
But I see the way you look at me
I know the way I look at you
Are we really just friends?

Wither:

My mom watched you wither away
She watched your sanity slowly slip away
She watched the wrinkles on your hands multiply

She saw all of the memories slowly start to fade away
She watched her best friend take her final breaths
She watched you die

Space and Time:

I want a love that transcends space and time
Something that makes the stars jealous and galaxies collapse
I want something that makes me feel everything all at once
Something that even the best composer can't even write about

All because what we have is more than anything anyone has seen before
I want something real and something that will last not just this lifetime
But all lifetimes
Something that brings gods to their knees

I want a love that makes me believe in miracles
Because when you found me I was at my lowest
You helped me grow higher than the heavens
And you helped me become the goddess I was always meant to be

Whipped Cream:

Two straws in a chocolate shake
Whipped cream on my nose
You leaned over the table and licked it off
While I giggled over your silliness

Holding hands on a hot summer day
Ice cream cones dripping down our hands
You picked my hand up and licked it off
And I giggled once more

Tickling each other on the couch
You pin me down and lick my face
I close my eyes and start giggling like always
When they open again, you're on one knee
With one motion you pulled out the most beautiful ring I'd ever seen

A year later and we're standing above a cake
I took your last name the way you took my heart
Each of us taking a bite and whipped cream ends up on your nose
I lick it off and you start giggling

Whipped cream isn't the sweetest thing
Because nothing compares to you

Sunflowers and Sadness:

Her smile was always pointed to the sun
Even with tears running down her face
She was and always would be made of
Sunflowers and Sadness

Happily Ever After:

I think the reason we become so sad growing up
Is because we realize that happily ever afters
Just don't come as easy as we were told

We realize that all of the hopes and dreams we had
Just aren't realistic
We aren't princes and princesses
We're the peasants
Broken, damned, hopeless
Some of us become the villans
But, we're all just average humans
Looking for some small glimmer of hope

Hope for a life that we've always wanted
Hope that one day we will get our happily ever after
Hope that we are enough

I think the reason we become so sad growing up
Is because we all start to realize
Happily ever afters just don't exist for all of us

Goodbye:

I remember it like it was yesterday
I had just talked to you the day before
We laughed and joked
The next day I got the call

I guess the sadness was too much
I guess it just became a weight too much to bear
I guess that you saw no hope anymore

I started thinking of all the times
You'd stop laughing for a few moments
As if the sadness crept back in and took over
Until you pushed it away to put back on the mask

I wish I had more time with you
I wish I could have taken this burden from you
I wish that I could say I love you one more time
I wish that I could have helped you

I guess this is me saying goodbye
I never got to say it to you
You were there one moment and gone then next
Before I could even realize what was happening

I want to hold you once more
To tell you everything was going to be okay
That although right now it hurts
There is a light at the end of the tunnel
I wish you told me
I would have sat in the darkness with you
Held your hand until you finally felt like fighting again
And then when you became weak again
I'd still be there to hold you hand

I guess this is my way of saying goodbye
I will always miss you and I will always love you

Heart:

Your initial still hangs around my neck
“Why?” my friends ask
Because even though our story is over
You still hold my heart

Forgive and Forget:

Why must I forgive and forget?
I would rather hate and remember
The anger inside of me
Keeps me going

It helps me become a better person than you
It reminds me to never believe a liar
The anger holds onto that hate
It shows me how I should be treated

The anger reminds me of who I am
Don't tell me that the anger is consuming me
I already know
But this hate inside of me keeps growing

It keeps going and going and going
It will one day destroy who I am
But that day will be the day
That I finally take my revenge

27

Growing up is like being stuck in a lion's den
With nothing but a twig to protect yourself
Like you're lost at sea
But all the rescue ships keep going in the wrong direction

I remember turning 21
Thought I knew everything there was to know
And here I am
So close to 27 and I realize I know nothing

My childhood is over
The toys locked away in the attic
The posters taken down
Memories of who I was… just gone

I try to relive my childhood
It's just not the same
Always feels like something is missing
And I think I know what

That little girl I used to be
Sitting outside on the playground
Swinging her feet of the ledge of the slide
Tears rolling down her face

Why is she crying?
You may ask
The truth is..
She had to grow up too fast

She never had a normal childhood
But here I am at 27
Holding that little girl close to my heart
Telling her that it's okay, she can rest now

www.ingramcontent.com/pod-product-compliance
Lightning Source LLC
LaVergne TN
LVHW050338160826
845677LV00014B/3682